DRAGON HILL

Gus the Mushroom Dragon

Read more Dragon Hill books!

DRAGON HILL

Gus the Mushroom Dragon

Written by
Tracey West
New York Times Bestselling
Author of Dragon Masters

Illustrated by
Carolina Vázquez

ACORN™
SCHOLASTIC INC.

In memory of Mrs. Bishop, the town librarian who supported and encouraged my love of reading when I was a kid. — TW

Para Mamá y Papá: Los quiero hasta el infinito y más allá. — CV

Library of Congress Cataloging-in-Publication Data

Names: West, Tracey, 1965– author | Vázquez, Carolina illustrator
Title: Gus the Mushroom Dragon / written by Tracey West ; illustrated by Carolina Vázquez.
Description: New York : Scholastic Inc, 2026. | Series: Dragon Hill ; 2 | Audience: Ages 5–7 | Audience: Grades K–1 | Summary: Gus the Mushroom Dragon uses his ability to connect with plants to rescue a new dragon friend and save a patch of flowers.

Subjects: CYAC: Dragons—Fiction | Ability—Fiction | Plants—Fiction | BISAC: JUVENILE FICTION / Readers / Chapter Books | JUVENILE FICTION / Social Themes / Friendship | LCGFT: Fantasy fiction
Classification: LCC PZ7.W51937 Gw 2026 | DDC [Fic]—dc23/eng/20250625
LC record available at https://lccn.loc.gov/2025002256

ISBN 978-93-5954-957-6

Printed in India at Sterling Graphics Pvt. Ltd Manesar

This reprint edition, March 2026

Edited by Katie Carella
Book design by Sarah Dvojack

Table of Contents

Forest
River Lena
Garden
Alden's Cave
Willow Pond
Meadow
Dragon Hill

Forest
Orchard
Singing Spring
Gus's Tree
Ember's Cave
Picnic Rock

Meet the Dragons!

Dragon Hill is a place filled with magic.
Many kinds of dragons live here.

Ember

Fact: She has lots of energy and ideas.
Dragon Type: Fire Dragon
Dragon Powers So Far: Making sparks

Gus

Fact: He likes rainy days and quiet spaces.
Dragon Type: Mushroom Dragon
Dragon Powers So Far: None yet

Mica

Fact: He lives underground.
Dragon Type: Rock Dragon
Dragon Powers So Far: Digging tunnels

Time to Practice

Gus the Mushroom Dragon lived in a big tree. One day, he and his family practiced their dragon powers.

His sister Gilly sprayed magical mist.
Her mist landed on some flowers.
The flowers grew bigger.

"You try, Gus!" Gilly said.

Gus closed his eyes.
He tried to make a mist.

Nothing happened.

"I can't do it," Gus said.

Next, his brother Gabe puffed up his body.
Gabe stepped off a tree branch.
He floated down to the ground.

"You try, Gus!" Gabe said.

Gus took a deep breath.
He tried to puff up his body.

Nothing happened.

"I can't do it!" Gus said.

He walked away.

Ember the Fire Dragon saw her friend Gus. "What is the matter, Gus?" she asked.

"I do not have any dragon powers yet," he said. "I'm sad."

"I understand how you feel," said Ember. "Watch this."

Ember scrunched up her snout. She snorted. Only sparks came out.

"I cannot breathe fire yet," said Ember. "But I will keep trying."

Gus smiled. "I will, too," he said. "One day, our powers will be strong."

A Strange Feeling

"Let's go to the apple orchard," Gus said to his best friend, Ember. "We can practice our powers there!"

"Great idea," Ember said. "We can snack on apples while we practice."

The friends walked along the path.

Suddenly, Gus stopped.
A strange feeling hit him.

"Someone in the orchard needs help!" Gus cried.

He started to run.

Ember caught up to her friend. "How do you know that someone needs help?" she asked.

"I am getting a strange feeling. This is new to me," Gus said. "The feeling seems to be coming from . . ."

Gus walked over to a flower patch.

"I think these flowers need help," Gus said.

"Hmm," Ember said. "The flowers **look** okay."

Gus touched the flowers.
"What is wrong?" he asked them.

The flowers sent him a scared feeling.

"They are scared," Gus told Ember.
"But I don't know why."

"Can you really understand the flowers?" Ember asked.

"Yes," Gus said. "I know that is strange."

"It is amazing," Ember said. "We will help these flowers together!"

A Monster?

The flowers in the orchard were scared.
Gus wanted to find out why.
He touched them again.

This time, Gus closed his eyes.

He saw pictures inside his head.
The flowers were sending him messages!

He saw the dirt under the flowers.

He saw the dirt shaking.

Then Gus heard a sound.

He opened his eyes.

Gus told Ember what he saw and heard.

"Wow!" Ember said. "I did not see anything. And you heard a growl?"

"Yes," Gus replied.

Ember looked scared. "Maybe there is a monster in the dirt!"

"We have to find out," Gus said. "How can we get under the flowers?"

Ember pointed. "I see a hole over there!"

They ran to the hole. It was next to a pile of dirt.

"I will go into the hole," Gus said. "I am just the right size."

"You are brave," Ember said. "I am afraid of the dark."

Gus climbed down. The hole led to a tunnel.

"Is that the monster?" he wondered.

Gus walked deeper into the tunnel.
He came to a wall of dirt.

Gus took a deep, brave breath.
"Hello, monster!" he cried.

A head pushed through the dirt!
Gus jumped. But it was not a monster.
It was a small Rock Dragon!

Mica

"My name is Mica," said the Rock Dragon.
"I was digging tunnels. Then I got turned around. Now I am tangled up in tree roots!"

"I'm Gus," Gus said. "Can you push your way out?"

"No. I am not strong enough," Mica replied.
"I am just a small Rock Dragon."

"You look big to me," Gus said.

"Gus, why did you think I was a monster?" Mica asked.

"I heard you growl," Gus said.

"I growl when I dig," Mica explained. "Like this."

Gus stepped back.

"Now I know why the flowers were scared," he said.

"Flowers can hear me?" Mica asked.

"Yes," Gus replied. "Your growl scared them."

"I did not mean to be scary," Mica said. "Can you help me get out of here?"

"I will be right back!" Gus said.

Gus climbed out of the hole.

Ember hugged him.

Gus told Ember about Mica.

"To help the flowers, we need to get Mica out of the tunnel," Gus said.

"Yes," Ember agreed. "We need to move the tree roots that are trapping him."

"The roots are thick," Gus said.

"How can we move them?" Ember asked.

Gus thought about the tree roots.
A big apple tree grew over Mica's tunnel.
"Those roots must belong to this tree,"
he said. "I know what to do!"

A Special Power

"We need to help Mica the Rock Dragon," said Ember.

"I have an idea!" Gus cried.

Gus touched the big apple tree.

"Hi there," Gus said. "I'm Gus. The flowers can hear me. Can you hear me, too?"

One tree branch moved up and down,
like it was nodding.

"Did the tree really hear you?" Ember asked. "That's so cool!"

"Can you please move your roots?" Gus asked the tree. "My friend Mica is trapped in them."

Ember and Gus waited.

The tree roots moved.

Mica was free!
He climbed out of the hole.

Mica shook off some dirt.

"Thank you both for helping me," he said. "And thanks, apple tree!"

Mica ran off.

"You have a special new power, Gus,"
said Ember. "You can connect with plants."

Gus smiled. "Thank you for helping me find my new power," he said.

Gus touched the flowers.
"Feel better now?" he asked.

The flowers sent him a happy feeling.

"Hooray!" said Gus.

About the Creators

Tracey West is the *New York Times* bestselling author of the Dragon Masters series. She loves to grow flowers and vegetables. She wishes Gus was around to help her understand them!

Carolina Vázquez is an Argentinian illustrator who enjoys creating images with cute characters and working with color and light to create artwork that brings the reader into the story. Along with creating art, Carolina enjoys swimming and spending time with her dog, Watson. She also loves reading novels and watching animated movies, which greatly inspire her work!

You Can Draw Gus!

1 Draw Gus's forehead, snout, mouth, and neck.

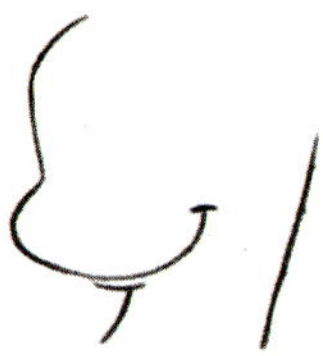

2 Add two ears.

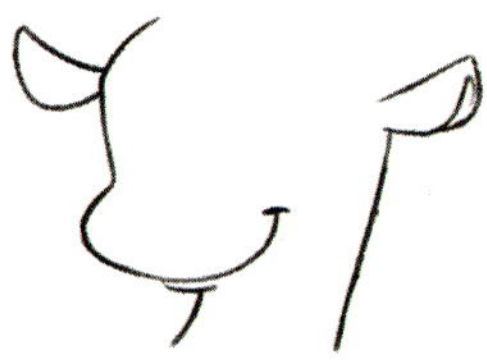

3 Give Gus a floppy-shaped head of hair.

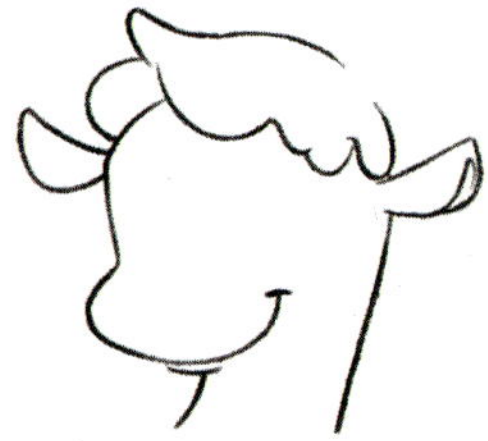

4 Add two mushroom-shaped horns on top of Gus's head. Draw two mini horns on his forehead. Then add two triangle-shaped horns on the back of his neck.

5 Add face details! Give Gus two eyes, eyebrows, nostrils, and teeth. Then draw two U-shaped scales and a vertical line along his neck.

6 Color in your drawing!

WHAT'S YOUR STORY?

Gus has the power to connect with plants.
Imagine that **you** are Gus the Mushroom Dragon.
What flower, tree, or other plant would send you a feeling?
How would you use your new power to help them?
Write and draw your story!

scholastic.com/acorn